secrets

I absolutely cannot keep a secret.
No matter how I try I always tell.
When I am told a secret
I really mean to keep it
To myself but I don't do so very well.

The very worst part of this whole problem,
That I wish I could be put on some back shelf,
Is that this terrible affliction
Seems to have no restrictions--
I even tell all secrets about myself!

hair

Some hair is nice and curly.
Some hair is nice and straight.
Then there's hair like mine
That doesn't look so great.

Like early in the morning
When I first awake
I could scare a very
Dangerous python snake.

I comb my hair so carefully
Every single day;
Still my hair insists
On going its very own way.

My dad says that I'm foolish
To even complain at all.
He just doesn't understand,
I guess because he's bald.

because

My mother said I must be good.
I told her I didn't know if I could.
She said that I had better try.
That is when I asked her, "Why?"

Inside her eyes I saw her smile
As she stared at me a long long while.
And just the way she always does,
She sighed a sigh and said, "Because."

never ending

Cups and saucers piled high –
Plates and platters to the sky –
Bowls of every size to do –
Seems as though I'm never through
Of washing, drying and putting away
Meal after meal, day after day.
If I were granted just one wish
It would be not to see another dish.
But since such wishes never come true,
Please excuse me – I have dishes to do.

no thanks!

Before we went to the restaurant
My parents said, "Listen, please.
Keep your elbows off the table
And your napkin on your knees.
Do no fooling with the silverware
And definitely no burping.
Sit up straight in your chair
And eat your soup without slurping.
Always take little bites.
Don't over butter your bread.
Now, on the way try to think
Of all the things we've said."
I was looking forward to eating out,
But I'm already starting to dread
Having so much to remember—
I think I'll just eat home instead

anticipation

In a tree they built their nest
Never taking time to rest.

Every twig was carefully placed,
Every intruder promptly chased.

Then mama took her royal seat,
And papa brought her things to eat,

Through the sunshine and the rain
Right outside my window pane.

patience

Waiting, waiting it's not easy
When the world is bright and breezy,
Knowing there are paths to travel,
Having secrets to unravel,

Baths to take in cooling puddles,
News to share in warming huddles.
Sitting, sitting undeterred,
How do you do it little bird?

circus time

It's like a circus in my back yard
And I have a front row chair
As I watch the squirrels run and jump
And go flying through the air.

They never miss each other's cues;
They're always ready and set.
And would you believe they do it all
Without a safety net?

busy

Busy, busy, busy, busy,
Busy little squirrel--
Running, skipping, jumping
Always in a dizzy whirl.
Stopping now and then to eat
A tasty little acorn treat--
Busy, busy, busy, busy,
Busy little squirrel.

squirrel tag

Run, run, chase!
Run, run, chase!
I see frisky squirrels
All over the place

Are playing tag
With one another
Across country roads,
One side to the other.

Scampering up trees
Flying out in space,
Loving every moment
Of danger that they face.

Scurrying through the eve troughs
Underneath the leaves,
Hardly ever seen
Making little bumps and heaves.

When the games are done
They hurry out of sight
Back to their cozy nests
To get ready for the night;

Until run, run chase!
Run, run chase!
Squirrels come playing tag
All over the place.

the picnic

The squirrels had a lovely picnic.
Miss McHugh said it was true.
They all gathered together
And had some acorn stew.

When the feast was over
Miss McHugh said, "Well, I guess
Those squirrels were just too tuckered out
To stay and clean the mess."

So we raked up all the leftovers,
Then sat a while to rest.
And we're sure we heard squirrels snoring
Way up high inside their nests.

19

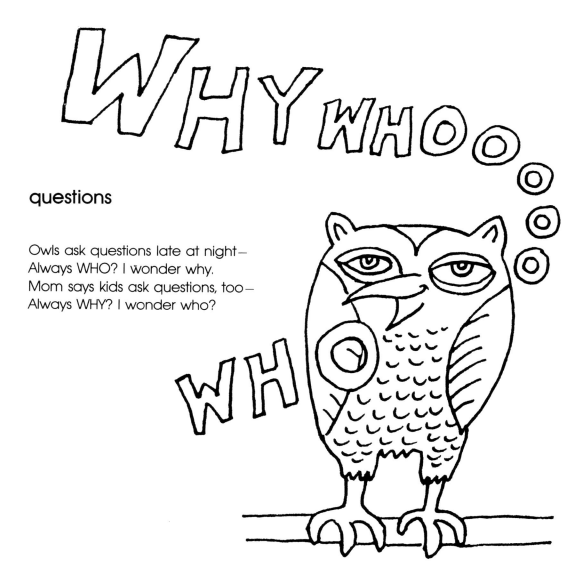

questions

Owls ask questions late at night—
Always WHO? I wonder why.
Mom says kids ask questions, too—
Always WHY? I wonder who?

silly fred

Silly Fred sleeps under his bed
And though his bones do ache,
He'd rather sleep under than in it
So his bed he won't have to make.

roses and noses

If roses were noses
And noses were roses
I'd send you some noses
To tickle your roses.

feet

Feet are such amazing things.
They can do most anything
Like walk, and hop, and skip, and run.
Dancing feet know how to have fun.

Young feet can be used all day.
Older feet, it's safe to say,
Occasionally need to rest
So they can do their every day best.

On ice feet like to slip and slide.
In sand feet dig and try to hide.
Puddles give feet a reason to splash.
Races give feet a reason to dash.

Feet like tapping to a beat
Or marching down a crowded street.
It's best for feet to go in pairs
Up and down long flights of stairs.

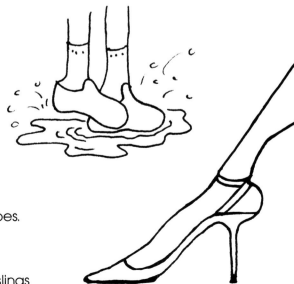

Quick feet can bring instant fame.
Slow feet can do quite the same.
And every ballerina knows
That feet must have ten good strong toes.

Jogging feet cover lots of ground.
Tiptoeing feet don't make a sound.
Bare footed, booted or in high heeled slings
Feet are such amazing things.

cookies cookies

Cookies! Cookies!
I love cookies!
I could eat cookies
All day long —
When I'm happy,
When I'm sad,
When I'm silly,
When I'm mad,
When I'm cold,
When I'm hot,
When I'm hungry,
When I'm not.
Chocolate double fudge,
Butterscotch crunch —
Cookies for breakfast
Dinner and lunch.
Strawberry marshmallows,
Peanut butter cream —
All night long
Of cookies I dream.
Give me cookies
Or a fuss I'll make.
What! No more cookies?
O.K. I'll take cake.

picky picky

There are special things I like to eat–
Not fish, not chicken not any meat.
But cereal that crackles, pickles that crunch,
Corn that goes POP, I like to munch.

As good as vegetables are supposed to be
Celery is the only one for me,
With bacon that sizzles, snaps and spits
And great big noisy potato chips.

Food that is quiet like spinach and peas,
Slippery custard, and smelly cheese,
Eggs and peanut butter, unless it's crunchy,
Are foods that never make me munchy.

Of course, whatever I'm given I eat
Whether sticky, mushy, sour, or sweet.
But let me make it perfectly clear –
I'm suspicious of food that I can't hear!

not my day

From the minute that I woke up,
I could tell it wasn't my day;
I couldn't do anything right,
And my mom had to go away.

Toothpaste got stuck all over.
Water leaked from the shower door.
With soapy eyes I grabbed for a towel
And knocked powder all over the floor.

Dad didn't have time to read me
The back of the cereal box;
He was searching all over the house
For a matching pair of his socks.

The toaster popped up burned toast.
The oatmeal was one awful lump.
Then Dad hit his head on the door
And gave himself a big bump.

My shirt went on kind of backwards.
There were knots in both shoe laces.
Dad got so upset when he saw
The bubble gum in my braces.

Kangaoo

My bus was the only one late,
Because it had a flat tire.
I was so hot all bundled up;
Boy, did I ever perspire!

When I finally got back home
I sat and fell asleep right there.
When I woke up I found my dad
Sound asleep in the other chair.

I can't wait for Mom to come home,
But there's something I have to say;
I hope she knows what she's doing
Bringing a baby here to stay!

I thought the worst was over,
Then Dad turned as white as a ghost
After he almost killed my cat
When he dropped a big frozen roast.

My mom forgot to leave money,
So I couldn't buy lunch today.
Dad forgot to write a note
Saying I could be in the play.

In spelling I couldn't remember
How to spell kangaroo.
In math I couldn't figure out
Twenty-one from forty-two.

best friend

I wish I had a best friend
To tell my secrets to.
Someone who would make me laugh
Whenever I feel blue.

Someone who could share my lunch,
Even my best dessert.
We'd have fun going around
Wearing each other's shirt.

We'd work and play together
And help each other out.
We'd never really argue
Like some who yell and shout.

Reading books with each other,
Making up silly rhymes
While munching crunchy cookies
Would be the best of times.

And climbing into bed
As each day reached its end,
I know that I'd sleep happy
Because of my best friend.

the fight

I had a fight with my best friend.
We called each other names.
She said that I was dumb in school.
I said she was awful at games.

She said I couldn't walk home with her.
I said that I didn't care.
But I really did, so I ran home fast
Right after I pulled her hair.

The next day in the school yard
She slapped me very hard.
That's when I made the terrible mistake
Of tearing her report card.

Her mother called my mother.
Then my mom called her mother, too.
I guess they both figured that is what
Good mothers were supposed to do.

We had a terrible fight,
But now we are good friends.
Isn't it strange how our mothers
Haven't talked to each other since then?

about sharing

I had a great big candy bar,
My friend asked me to share.
I wouldn't, even when she cried,
And said I didn't care.

I wanted it all for myself,
So I didn't let her,
But now I think if I had shared
It would have tasted better.

silly talk

Grown-ups say such silly things
Like "Sit down and sit up",
Or "Would you like a glass of milk?",
Then hand out milk in a cup.
I hope that I remember
To do better when I'm grown
But I have a funny feeling
I'll say silly things of my own.

enough!

Good-bye Mom. I'm going out now.

       Have fun and don't be late.

O.K. I'll be home by eleven.

       Oh, no! You'll be home by eight.

How about if I get here by ten?

       How about if you get here by nine?

What about good old nine-thirty?
Don't you think that sounds just fine?

       Nine fifteen is the limit
       And be here on the dot!

Thanks! I knew you'd come through, Mom,
But nine-twenty would sure hit the spot!!

surprise

Dad, I got my liscence!

       Of course, I knew you would.

I followed every traffic sign.

       Just the way you should.

I made a perfect three point turn.

       I always knew you could.

Dad, Can I take the car tonight?
Dad, you don't look so good!

31

ant watching

I was watching some ants the other day
Not knowing if they were at work or play.
They just kept moving constantly
Which was absolutely amazing to see.
They crawled along at quite a pace
As if taking part in a relay race.
And I observed that actually
Ants are busier, by far, than bees.

bugs

Don't you think bugs are wonderful
The way they crawl around
Making people yell and scream
And jump up off the ground?
Most people are such 'fraidy-cats
It's very plain to see.
What?
You say there's a WHAT?
A yeeOOOOOOOOOOW!
Make way! There's a bug on me!

annoyance

It's amazing to me
How a little flea
Makes me jump about the house.

More amazing to me
Is that I usually can't see
The annoying little louse.

33

machines

Our house is filled with eating machines,
The finest machines that have ever been seen.
One especially likes dirt from the floors.
One gobbles food as it bellows and roars.

Another lives on a diet of trash.
One big gulp turns trash into mash.
A little machine that hangs on the wall
Loves snacking on treats considerably small.

Outside our house the feasting goes on
With dining machines to climb upon
That chew tall grass until none can be seen.
There's even a gourmet leaf eating machine.

Do beware for one could get hurt
By ravenous diners gobbling rocks and dirt.
Turning its stomach is how the day's spent
By a machine that craves the taste of cement.

It seems that people who lived long ago
Would most certainly be surprised to know
About these diners they'd never seen.
But that would require a time eating machine!

drippy

slurpy

sticky

gooey

the mess

drippy . . .
slurpy
sticky
gooey

Clean up that mess!!

Phooey!

singing

It's fun to sing all through the day
When I work or when I play.
Going to school or in the shower
I could sing non-stop by the hour.

I'll sing to the mud and to the snow,
To falling rain and flowers that grow.
I'll sing to leaves that fall from trees.
I'll sing along with any old breeze.

I'll serenade places near and far
And every little shining star.
At the table or in my bed,
Right side up or on my head,

Every morning, noon and night,
Softly or with all my might.
But one thing that is definitely true—
I like singing best with you.

ring   do-be-do

sh oo

zip

be-do   wa

hmm

rock concert

I love to sing with the radio
While riding along in a car.
I pretend I'm a famous rock singer
Playing my twelve-string electric guitar.

I imagine I'm wearing fancy clothes
With beads that shine like gold.
And I sing high notes that for anyone else
Are impossible to hold.

I plan what I'll say when I'm interviewed
On radio and T.V.,
Then I'm rushed by my fans for my autograph
Like a famous celebrity.

When I run on stage to the cheering crowd
I'm the best and most famous rock star
That ever gave a sell out performance
While riding along in a car.

musical sounds

Bop bop-de-bop bop bop
Zip zippity zing
Shoo shoo-be--do wawa
Ring ring-a-ling ling

La la-de-da da da
Ching ching-a-ching chong
Hm hm-hm-hm hm hm
I do-be-do love that song!

january 2nd

January 2nd is not so bad
For all the kids who have ever had
To go back to school to learn new things
Like history, math, and songs to sing.

It's the one day no one's ever late,
For seeing friends is always great.
Telling of the holiday fun –
The parties, the gifts, and the games that were won.

And though the new year brings work to do
That seems impossible to ever get through,
Kids will usually say, "Let's try it,"
While parents go on their same old diets.

mom

I woke up to the strangest sounds
And when I went to see,
I found my mom in a sweat suit
In front of our T.V.

She was bending and stretching quickly
To the count of 1,2,3,4.
So busy trying to keep in step,
She never noticed me at the door.

I was really surprised to witness
The things my mom could do,
But I got a little worried
When her face went from red to blue.

She huffed and puffed and grunted
But never did she stop,
Not even when a voice said,
"Now let's take it again from the top!"

I went to my room and dressed
Then went to the breakfast table.
I was shocked to find Mom cooking,
Never dreaming that she'd be able.

I didn't mention what I had seen.
Mom never mentioned it either.
I could tell from the look that was on her face
She was happy to have a small breather.

When I told my friend all about it
She said she believed it was true.
Then she laughed and said the very same thing
Was going on at her house, too!

just in time

When the moon is staring
And the wind is howling
My imagination
Starts its prowling

Into corners dark
And noises scary
Until I see monsters
Tall and hairy

With green glowing eyes
And breath of fire.
I feel as though
I'll surely expire.

When just as I am
About to give in
Across my face
I feel a big grin.

It's amazing to me
And I'd like to know
How my imagination
Knows just how far to go.

40

mud

I love the feel of mud
As it squishes in my hands,
Sneaks out between my fingers,
Dribbles down my arms, and lands

Upon the ground in blobs
That quickly turn to fun
As my imagination
Begins to wildly run.

Faces soon appear –
Some very old, some young,
Elephants, mice, and tiny ants
In rows so neatly strung.

Sometimes I see dinosaurs
And face them eye to eye.
It's a little like making pictures
Out of clouds up in the sky.

And though I can spend hours
In mud, I can't deny
I wish I could turn mud pies
Into pumpkin pie.

vacation

It's fun to go on vacation
If you go by train or jet,
But when you go by car
Very bored is what you get.

You hope to make the time pass
By trying to read a book,
But the words jump around,
Making it difficult to look.

Then you whistle a catchy tune
Or try humming a little hum.
Finally you blow some bubbles
With your favorite bubble gum.

No matter what you try to do
Nothing seems to work.
If you don't think of something fast
You will surely go berserk.

As desperation starts to grow
You suggest a trivia game
Or giving just initials
And guessing somebody's name.

That lasts about five minutes
Then you're back where you began
Trying to find something to do
To pass the time if you can.

Counting cars and animals
Can only take you so far.
So you use the best excuse
A few times to stop the car.

Someone suggests the radio,
But that never turns out right.
Everyone wants their own station
And that means a great big fight.

I still like to go on vacation,
And when we go the next time
I will probably pass the hours
With another silly rhyme.

history

History is and that's because
History is the way that it was.
History can be yesterday
Or long ago and far away.

Alexander was still a kid
When he accomplished all he did.
And that young Queen Elizabeth the First
On survival was so well versed.

The Roman Empire cracked and fell.
Those Romans didn't do too well.
Bold Napoleon never knew
He wouldn't survive Waterloo.

The North and South fought day and night
Defending what each thought was right.
Marie Antoinette's big mistake
Was when she said, "Let them eat cake."

It's fun to study kings and queens
And famous people in between;
But history is at its best
When you don't have to take a test.

spring

The breeze feels it
And tries to steal it.

The flowers know it
And start to grow it.

The birds wing it
And sweetly sing it.

Just what is it?
IT'S SPRING!

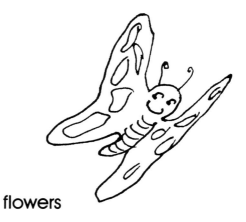

flowers

Flowers make me happy.
Flowers make me glad.
Flowers always cheer me up
Whenever I feel sad.

I see the lovely colors
And sniff each gentle scent.
The time I spend with flowers
Is time, I think, well spent.

rain song

The gentle rain came softly at first,
But knowing of the ground's mighty thirst
Soon started falling hard and fast
Giving nourishment that would last

When raindrops would no longer fall.
But, oh, you see that is not all,
For I heard the rain upon the roof
And that was very definite proof

That rain does more than simply fall;
Rain makes music best of all.
Whether soft and gentle, hard and strong,
Each rainfall sings a fresh new song.

quiet thoughts

The hot sun smiles friendly smiles
On roads that beckon for many miles.
The distant moon in solitude thinks
As the thirsty ground eagerly drinks.
Mellow frogs whisper soft and low
To stars that flirt as they warmly glow.
Leaves in chorus proudly sing
To snowflakes that flutter like butterfly wings.
And owls ask questions late at night
For answers that are out of sight.

45

make room

If you always keep a poem close by
You'll never feel alone –
Like when you're waiting for a bus,
Or your turn to use the phone.

A poem can keep you from being bored,
Or help you to fall asleep,
Especially when you run out of numbers
Needed for counting sheep.

A poem doesn't really have to have
Much time in which to fit.
Usually it takes only seconds
To recall the whole of it.

Poems can be written, read or said.
There are poems you can almost eat.
All poems have a built in rhythm.
Each one has its very own beat.

People you know, places you go
And all the feelings you feel
Are the ingredients you will need
To make your poems feel real.

So, standing, sitting, working, playing
Or on your way to bed,
You'll always have time for a poem or two
If you keep a few in your head.

the sound of rain is definitely red

What color is the sound of rain
Bouncing off your window pane,
Or briskly marching across a road
Before swirling down a waiting drain?

What color is the beat of drops
Hitting high roofs in skips and hops,
Rolling to the edge and falling below
Onto quickly passing umbrella tops?

What color is the melody
That splashes into the open sea
Then rushes to the waiting shore
To push and pull you playfully?

Now, listen carefully — don't be led
Into hearing blue or gray instead
Of hearing from the very first drop
That the sound of rain is definitely red.

47

index